Big Bands and Small Farms

Big Bands and Small Farms

Don R. Krohn, M.D.

2010

To my wife, Betty

***

Contents

Acknowledgments

Thank you to all the family members who offered encouraging words and support while I wrote this book. I would especially like to thank my son-in-law Steve Shegedin, who worked with me continuously on this project—helping coordinate the photographs and the text, contributing various honest thoughts to the development of the stories, and offering very pertinent observations as we reviewed the material together. Also, thank you to the residents and staff at Farmington Square. Your support, friendship, and encouragement in my writing pursuits have been greatly appreciated. Thanks also to Kate for her editorial assistance, to Aliesia and Heather for typing up my transcriptions in the earliest phase of this project, and to those friends who dropped in or called, listened to my stories in progress, and even laughed at my jokes (especially Clif). It seems appropriate as well to thank those friends and acquaintances who appear in the stories themselves—thank you for being a part of my life story. Finally, a thank you to Peg Goldstein, aka Phelps, for her contribution as editor.

Introduction

This is the second book I've written from an assisted-living facility in Eugene, Oregon. Like my first book, *Tap Dancing, Babies, and Cadavers: Humor and Pathos in the Life of a 20th-Century Doctor*, this new collection of stories recounts my life before I was diagnosed with Parkinson's disease.

In my ten-year history with the disease, my symptoms have gradually worsened, though I still remain somewhat active and get around with the help of a walker or wheelchair. Medications have helped with the disease. While I've experienced some degree of debilitation, my symptoms are largely under control. Despite these obstacles, my writing seems to me to be quite acceptable, but then, perhaps I am prejudiced.

One of my motivations for writing a second book was to have focused mental activity with a plan for completion. I think Parkinson's patients can help themselves by having goals. In the assisted-living facility, I've noticed that the residents who are active with projects seem to do better.

Moreover, I wrote this second book because writing the first book was such a good experience. One of the best and unexpected benefits that came from the first publication was the rekindling of old friendships. I reconnected with friends who were mentioned in the book—most of whom I hadn't talked with in decades. I've also appreciated the positive comments from my friends and others who enjoyed the book. Writing a book, though a difficult process, has been rewarding for me.

All things considered, my life has been pleasant and continues to be pleasant due to many things, including my family and friends. I feel quite optimistic about the future.

—Don Krohn
Eugene, Oregon
October 2010

Big Bands

As a high school student in the mid-1940s, I was privileged to hear many concerts by the big bands. Students paid a reduced rate to hear the highest-quality musical programs, primarily at the Downtown Theater in Detroit, Michigan. We also heard big bands over the radio, in movies, on records, and at open-air concerts. The bands included some of the finest musicians of all time, such as Jimmy and Tommy Dorsey, Benny Goodman, Glenn Miller, Artie Shaw, Count Basie, Harry James, Woody Herman, Duke Ellington, Cabell "Cab" Calloway, Les Brown, Gene Krupa, Kay Kyser, Lionel Hampton, Lawrence Welk, Stan Kenton, and Lindley Armstrong "Spike" Jones. These musicians were renowned worldwide and played music that has not been equaled since. Their sound embraced the intimacy and excitement of the era.

The bands had an interesting way to keep costs down. The band director, along with four or five key musicians, traveled from town to town. In each town, this core group recruited local professional musicians into their ranks. This saved money on transportation costs, lodging, and food. The sound of the performance stayed the same no matter what town it was heard in. Under the leadership of the band director and the key musicians, the talented local musicians could accurately render the band's unique orchestrations, captured in sheet music.

Special attention should be paid to Lawrence Welk, who crossed my path in many ways. He often came to Bloomfield, Nebraska, my hometown, to play music on Saturday nights at the local fairgrounds. His humble beginnings included participation in a three-piece band, in which he was the accordionist. His apprenticeship extended more than twenty years. He earned a reputation for providing very satisfying "champagne music" for adults, who primarily danced to it and had marvelous times. Welk went on to television, where he became a nationally known figure. His young audience propelled his fame as they grew to be adults. The adult fans shared Welk's music with their own children.

Lawrence Welk

During the big band era, I was caught up in the cultural change. I carried my trombone case on the bus, making sure that others could see the "Les Brown Band of Renown" logo on the side. Although I played in the high school band and orchestra, I was never considered a competent musician.

"Fourth trombone you are flat, flat, flat!" my director would scream. "Can't you hear it?"

"No sir, I can't," I replied.

"Well, then, maybe you should blow the spit out of your instrument more frequently!"

From that moment on, I was known as Juicy Tone Krohn on the Slide Trombone.

Tommy Dorsey, a leader of the big band sound

Don R. Krohn, M.D.

As a special tribute, I would like to recognize a friend, George Hastings. At age sixty-five, he has been a performer and drum teacher for fifty-plus years. He sat in with the Scoby Big Band in major cities across the United States. He played with John Lee Hooker's blues band, among others. Presently, George teaches drumming by demonstration, after the manner of his mentor, Dave Black. He has his own band and attempts to preserve the style and tradition of his late teacher. He currently has three drumming students. George also works the night shift at my assisted-living facility, where he can be heard tapping rhythms with his hands and fingers—in infinite variations and to his heart's content. *He drums while others sleep.*

George Hastings

Brewery Workers of America

When I was nineteen years of age and on summer vacation between my freshman and sophomore years in college, I was a member of the Brewery Workers of America. At that time, in 1948, Detroit had six or seven breweries. The breweries had full-time employees but needed additional seasonal help, since people drank more in the summertime. Many people thought of beer as a cooling beverage.

We seasonal workers reported to a designated area each day, and a boss would announce how many extra employees the company needed. You had to show up frequently to get anything close to a consistent job assignment.

I started out as an inspector, checking bottles. The job involved viewing each bottle through a large magnifying glass as it moved along the line. Because many of the bottles were reused, there was always a chance that former owners had left—or intentionally placed—miscellaneous objects in them. Occasionally, I'd find a grasshopper, roach, mouse, or chewing gum. (Incidentally, experienced beer drinkers of the time always held their full bottles up to the light to check for foreign objects.) I also watched for occasional broken bottles. Before passing my inspection station, bottles went single file along the conveyor through the washer, filler, capper, and pasteurizer. After my station, I watched the bottled beer go to the caser, out to the floor, and out the door.

Later that summer, my main job was to stack cases of beer in multiple locations within an extensive warehouse. Trucks would pull out fully loaded, headed toward New York City, Toronto, Chicago, and elsewhere. We would keep the beer as fresh as possible by taking the most recent batch to the end of the line for loading. Three people did all the stacking of the cased beer.

I worked with two gentlemen consistently. One of them, Elmer, was of Swedish extraction. He would give us almost indecipherable signals about where we were supposed to work next. When we couldn't find the spot, he would say in his distinctive Swedish accent, "Well, boys, I think we should go back to where we was before." This line used to crack us up, except that by then we'd be a full truckload or so behind schedule.

We sometimes drank on the job, and the best beer was beer that had not gone through the pasteurization process. Many people questioned the sobriety of the workers. You could drink all the beer you could handle, but if you showed any sign of drunkenness you were laid off immediately—since the brewery was concerned about liability. The men I met were like any other group of men. Some drank a good amount of beer, while others drank only on occasion. At the end of shifts, we sat on benches outside the brewery and had a beer or two.

During that time, President Harry Truman was running for a second term in office. He made a big speech at City Hall. Thousands of people gathered on bleachers to hear him. People filled the streets and had a huge parade. For this event, my bosses at the brewery gave me a great honor. I was chosen to carry the flag for the Brewery Workers of America. Marching down the street, I led the parade. I liked doing my part to support the president, and I enjoyed all the people clapping and carrying on for us brewery workers. Afterward, my coworkers and I retired to the union hall and had a beer or two. After that summer, I never worked in a brewery again, but I remember it as one of the most pleasant times of my life.

"Hello"

Bill Feltner and I were undergraduates at Wayne State University in Detroit in the late 1940s. We were both on a premedical curriculum, and we graduated at the same time. We became quite close as undergraduates. We did numerous things together, including picnics, excursions in open country, outings on Belle Isle, and other pleasurable activities with our girlfriends, Betty and Barbara.

At the time, I worked part-time as a Fuller Brush salesman. This was a commissioned sales job. One day I suggested to Bill that he join the company so we could work as partners. Like me, Bill considered Fuller Brush products to be fine merchandise, and he agreed to join me in the Fuller Brush operation. But before Bill joined me in the partnership, I needed to teach him the ropes for several weeks.

At a Fuller Brush convention, the company president announced that we two college students were now Fuller Brush Men. Also at the convention, we established our partnership and sang a song dedicated to the Fuller Brush Company: "Pack up your brushes in your little black bag and sell, sell, sell." After the convention, we took the Fuller Brush motto with us and went about our business.

We were assigned a section of selling territory close to Wayne State. It extended from Detroit's east side, on Fifth Street, to Woodard Avenue in the middle of the city. This section was about five blocks wide and three miles deep and consisted primarily of apartment dwellers. Our routine was to distribute a vegetable brush and catalog to each potential customer and then make an appointment for a private session at a later date. We never knew what we would run into on the job.

Bill and I once presented a toilet brush to a group of ladies. We told the ladies all about the brush. We told them how it was made of the best materials and how they could repeatedly use it with no difficulties. I presented the brush as durable by standing on it with one heel, bearing all my weight on it while spinning around 360 degrees. I then tapped the brush against my knee— at which point all the bristles fell out. We all laughed about it and continued on with our presentation.

Bill became quite well known to the people in the Fuller Brush operation when he made the largest sale anyone in the company had ever made during his first solo sales call. He called on a room full of deaf individuals, who were pleased about having a nice-looking young man treat them with respect and were pleased to receive free vegetable brushes. The big sale was called to the attention of authorities in the organization.

Bill was now a confident Fuller Brush Man, and he went out on his own. He was walking in the second-floor hallway in one of the many apartment dwellings we dealt with when he heard someone say, "Hello."

"Hello," Bill called out.

"Hello, hello, hello," he heard in response.

The door was slightly ajar. Bill pushed it open and said, "Hello."

Again a response came: "Hello. Hello. Hello."

He noticed a door on the other side of the apartment—possibly a bedroom. This second door was also ajar. Bill opened it and said, "Hello?" He saw a bed and a dresser. This was indeed a lady's bedroom. But the lady of the house was nowhere in sight.

He heard the voice again: "Hello." Bill looked in the corner of the room. There he saw a large green parrot with a preoccupied expression, sitting on a perch. "Hello. Hello. Hello," said the bird.

As Bill made his discovery, the lady of the apartment came into the bedroom and shrieked, "What are you doing in my bedroom?!"

Bill, always thinking quickly, said, "I am your Fuller Brush Man."

Don Krohn and Bill Feltner, intrepid Fuller Brush Men,
confident in the value of their product

A Diamond Ring

Betty and I met at a party in Detroit in October 1949. We went together for quite a long spell and in June 1951 became engaged to be married. I thought it would be appropriate to buy her an engagement ring. At the time, I was working as a laboratory technician in a Detroit hospital. I knew a man, who knew a guy, who had a friend, who was more or less a jeweler by avocation.

This fellow, I was told, carried around a canvas bag filled with diamonds. His name was Jack Ace. After I got in touch with the fellow, I made an appointment to meet him.

I found Jack's diamond business without any difficulty. When he opened the door to let me into his place, I had the surprise of my life—when two large and rather nervous monkeys greeted me at the door. They both jumped on me and climbed from one of my shoulders to the other. "WHOO-HO, WHOO-HO-AH, AH-AH-AHHH," they cried. One of the monkeys grabbed a large chandelier that hung in the dining area and swung across the room. "WRRAAAAW!" cried one of the pair, as it jumped from the floor and banged its fists against the wall.

"Get down, Bob! Settle down, Stan!" Jack yelled to the monkeys, trying to call them off. They continued to make the crazy noises as if they were very angry—and they made crazy faces to match. He finally did settle them down, and these crazed monkeys reluctantly came under control.

After composing himself, Jack described the diamond that I was considering purchasing. He said it was larger than a half karat. He explained to me that all diamonds had imperfections and the fewer the "bubbles," as he called them, the more valuable the diamond. We agreed upon a price of $300.

Many years later, a string of Betty's pearls broke. We took the pearls to a jeweler in Ann Arbor to be repaired. As part of his service, he agreed to appraise Betty's diamond ring. We were curious to see what kind of deal I had made many years earlier with the diamond dealer in Detroit. The Ann Arbor jeweler appraised the diamond at $1,125, not including the setting. When all was said and done, I was very pleased with the deal I had made on Betty's ring. But I could have done without the monkeys.

Betty and I on our wedding day, August 11, 1951

Footlocker Intrigue

I first met Don Burgess in 1959. We were both captains in the U.S. Air Force and had just flown from an airfield on the East Coast to Rhein-Main, Germany. We were seated on a bus for an approximately three-hour drive to Bitburg Air Force Base, where I was beginning a two-year tour of duty. We got to know each other well.

Each of us was assigned to Bitburg Hospital. Burgess was the new supply officer, and I was an obstetrics and gynecology specialist. I enjoyed working with Burgess, who was a very cheerful person and quite familiar with air force regulations. He had come up in the ranks. We discussed a host of issues and got together at the officer's club for dinner the day we arrived.

In the morning, we met at the hospital with our commander, Colonel Morris. After introducing himself, Morris assigned duties to each of us. Mine was to serve as a physician in labor and delivery and to provide every married serviceman with a cuckoo clock and a new baby. Colonel Morris laughed and explained that it was not a very complex assignment, but I would have a lot of responsibility. I was working for the well-being of six thousand U.S. citizens at the air force base, as well as people in various embassies, including those of Belgium and Holland.

Morris turned to me and said, "Captain Krohn, you have this well in mind, and I will not bother you any further with it. I wish you good luck, and if there is anything that I can do to make your task easier, please do not hesitate to ask. We are here to serve the air force and our country, and that is responsibility enough."

"Now Captain Burgess," he said as he turned his attention to Don, "you have a more difficult duty. We have been confronted with a problem that requires the patience of Job. We sent a requisition for fifty footlockers through the command structure of Europe and finally to the Pentagon. It appears that during those steps of requisition, two zeros were added to the order, leading to a total of five thousand footlockers."

Colonel Morris went on to explain that we needed only fifty footlockers for the fifty corpsmen living across from the hospital. These corpsmen performed practical procedures on routine lacerations, cuts, and small burns. Within a few minutes, they could get to a patient's bedside or to the lab to provide whatever nursing care might be required.

We were dumbfounded to learn what had happened. Indeed, a zero had been added twice to the requisition as it passed through various hands. The factory providing us with the footlockers went on a third shift. It was able to get the British to decommission an outmoded battleship. This humble structure was reserved for an indefinite period to store the five thousand footlockers. However, due to a tactical problem, this arrangement didn't last very long. Finally a warehouse was built in Bremerhaven to house the footlockers. We could remove only one footlocker at a time, since our command was limited primarily to F-100s, small military fire bombers.

I met with Don Burgess many times at meals. He kept me up to date on the situation with the footlockers. He was still working on the problem after two years, when my tour of duty was complete.

I have made it a project to find out what ever happened to the footlockers. I looked it up on the Internet and in various other sources provided by the air force itself, but apparently no one knows what finally happened.

Whose Milk?

During our stay in Germany, when I was a captain in the air force, my wife and I rented a second-floor apartment in the city of Trier. At the time we had three young children, Bill, Vicki, and David. Besides playing with their toys, they loved to play one of our only records, Fats Domino's "I'm Gonna Be a Wheel Someday." As the song played, the kids formed a parade. Bill was the parade master, followed by Vicki, who pushed David in the stroller. Over and over, for hours it seemed, they played the song—singing along and marching around the dining table.

The three children also spent their time drinking copious amounts of milk. We wanted the freshest possible milk, so we ordered it directly from the dairy, which agreed to deliver it fresh to our doorstep. We contacted our landlady, Frau Heinz, to assist us with the arrangements.

Frau Heinz was a nice, businesslike woman in her forties. She lived above us on the third floor of the building. She always wore her hair in a tight bun. Like Betty and I, Frau Heinz believed that milk was a healthful beverage for young children to drink. Without hesitation, she placed our order for fresh bottles of whole milk, which was to be delivered to our house on a routine basis. Frau Heinz was very helpful throughout the series of problems that soon erupted.

A month later, we received a steep bill for the milk delivery charges. We were very surprised, since we had not received any milk. Our landlady checked with the dairy, which claimed to have been sending out milk. Then she went to the police station to report the problem. The police referred us to the local magistrate, Herr Dunkle. He asked many questions and looked into the situation thoroughly. Finally, he replied, "Well, placing anything on the stoop of the house, where this milk was delivered, does not indicate ownership of that item."

He went on to explain that while it was true that ownership had been transferred in the dairy manager's department, it was not clear whether or not we owned the milk when it was left on the stoop, which was deemed public property.

"The milk is nobody's milk," he declared. He explained that because the milk had not fallen into the right hands or been transferred at the proper location, there was nothing he could do. Had the milk been placed on the exit or entrance of the stoop, he explained, we might have had a claim. But since no such place existed, anything left on the stoop belonged to nobody.

Herr Dunkle crossed his arms across his chest. He smiled smugly. "You see, it is just the same as a ship abandoned on the high seas. It is nobody's ship!"

Frau Heinz responded, "We shall see about that!"

That night Frau Heinz set her alarm clock for an hour earlier than usual. In the morning, she waited just inside the front door of the building to see the milk delivered. The milkman arrived on schedule and placed our milk on the stoop. Immediately after he drove off, a boy of about eleven walked up, took the milk in his arms, and strolled away. Not missing a beat, Frau Heinz ran after the boy and made it clear to him that the milk was our milk and not up for grabs.

To settle the issue once and for all, she continued to get up an hour early every day and await the arrival of the milkman, who handed the milk to her directly. Thus possession passed clearly from the dairy, or its agent, to Frau Heinz, our agent.

After this intervention, we had no problem obtaining our milk. Our landlady saved the day by untangling us from confusing German ownership laws, which continue to be a mystery to me.

The copious milk drinkers, Bill, Vicki, and David, in Germany on Christmas Eve, 1959

Murray Deighton

Murray Deighton and I enjoyed many good times together. We also collaborated on projects related to the departments and the executive committee of the hospital where we both worked. For most of the time I knew him, Murray was chairman of the hospital's Family Practice Department. He was well thought of in family practice affairs because he had an active, very viable residency program.

He and I met when a professor named Creeser gave an orientation lecture on our first day as premed students at Wayne State. Dr. Creeser noted that of the six thousand freshman students in undergraduate studies, four thousand were hoping to get into medical school. Dr. Creeser said, "Fellows, look around you. Because of the dropout rate and the change in attitudes toward the completion of a degree, the man sitting at your left or your right should have some concern. One of them will be absent next year if the present trend continues."

Murray and I looked at each other and laughed. I can't tell you why we thought it was so funny, but we did.

We both went on to medical school. Wayne State graduated Murray at the same time I graduated from the University of Michigan. Murray went on to a family practice residency program, and I went on to a residency program in OB-GYN. We both became certified in our fields.

Interestingly, when we went into practice, we unknowingly rented houses with adjoining backyards. I had four children, and I believe Murray had six.

Don R. Krohn, M.D.

One day we were conversing on the steps of the Detroit Public Library. We were engaged deeply in conversation when a man came forward and said:

Pardon me boys, I can't help but be interested in your conversation. I enjoy the way you are bringing out these main points, and I hope you won't mind me entering into your discussion. You see, I am looking for the details with which we can replicate a gyroscopic compass that I think will help us in our quest. We intend to mount a second expedition this summer, when we will once again look for the entrance to the Garden of Eden. You may have heard that we had no success with our last expedition, but I think the gyroscopic compass will help us. We owe this to the Detroit Library because it was so generous in allowing me to research this compass and its engineering details. Last summer we found what we thought was the entrance to the Garden of Eden. We lowered the captain's son into this great hole in the western provinces of Canada and never saw him again.

At this point it was apparent that the gentleman was highly delusional—or "world-class" delusional as our friend Jack Pfeifer would have said. In any case, the man was dressed in all white. He wore a white shirt, tie, vest, and pants. He had a white suit coat to match. He wore a white hat and white shoes with white stockings. He was truly an apparition in white, and upon seeing this gentleman, you would be impressed. He went on to tell us about his quest, his captain's logs, and his plans for the second expedition. This man was truly a sight to behold.

Murray had a great sense of humor. He said to me one day, "There have been so many things we have done together, Krohn, that I am overwhelmed when I think about it. We have served nearly fifteen years on the executive committee at the hospital. We've finished up the training of a number of good doctors in our specialty practices. We've had social contact throughout the nearly fifteen years that we have been associated. It has been a really productive life. The only thing that can top it would be if we both were to die in a head-on automobile crash." Then he laughed the small chuckle that showed he was really amused and that you knew him very well. Murray had a presence that could be felt.

I was privileged to give something of a eulogy when Murray Deighton did pass away. He has truly been missed.

Suburbia

It was about 10:30 p.m. in the summer of 1964, and we were getting settled in at our new home in suburbia. The previous week, we had moved from a rental to our own home in Farmington Hills, a suburb of Detroit.

Suddenly there was a pounding on our front door. There was a group of about twenty to twenty-five people outside. When we opened the door, they all came into the house. They were there to throw us a party, they said. They had brought along beer and food. Among the partygoers were Dwight and Alma Nash, the only people I knew in the group. We never found out who had organized the party.

Things were going pretty well. One guest gave a welcoming speech. People were relaxed. As it approached eleven o'clock, there was a sudden banging noise.

"It sounded like a cannon went off," my son David said. It brought the party to a screeching halt. We listened and moments later heard the sound of a screaming woman. She was yelling at the top of her voice. She was apparently trapped in the bathroom.

We rushed to the door and opened it. To our surprise, we found a large lady, apparently in great pain, lying crossways in the bathtub. She was obscurely bent at the middle of her back and wedged into the bathtub in a peculiar manner. Her legs were straight up in the air, and her girdle was around her knees. She was quite stuck in this painful position.

Several male partygoers, including myself, attempted to assist this woman out of the bathtub, but she was wedged in too tightly and grotesquely. We wondered if we needed to call an ambulance.

But finally, our group figured out how to help the woman. Two men held onto each of her legs, while another man lifted her shoulders. Together they managed to hoist her out of the bathtub.

Several ladies took an interest in the case and brought the woman a glass of water. She soon settled down. She explained that she had fallen into the bathtub while trying to pull her girdle up after using the restroom. Apparently, she had lost her balance, twisted 90 degrees, and fallen backward into the tub.

Nobody at the party knew who she was. Nobody recognized her, and she didn't announce her name. Nobody could guess what she was doing at a party where nobody knew her. It was a quite an unusual experience.

Game Ball

It was bitterly cold and windy on Thanksgiving Day at Detroit's Briggs Stadium in 1962. My friend Jim Spence (whom I had known since 1948, when we were in the same English class at Wayne State) and I were bundled up and ready for a good game.

The Green Bay Packers included six future Hall of Famers, including Coach Vince Lombardi. We knew that the Detroit Lions were likely to take a fall that day. The Packers were coming into Detroit with ten wins and no losses that season. They were the prohibitive favorites. They had the best coach in football, the best running back, the best offensive line, and one of the best quarterbacks, Bart Starr. Coach Lombardi had stated that this particular Packers team was the best he had ever seen.

Well, let's just say things didn't go as expected. Before 57,598 fans at Briggs Stadium and a national television audience, the Lions sacked Starr eleven times that day for a total loss of 110 yards. Lion defensive lineman Roger Brown played the best game of his long career. Alex Karras joined Brown in controlling the Packers' offense.

From our end zone seats, we were very close to the players as they trotted off the field at halftime. Packer center lineman Jim Ringo staggered off the field—evidence that he had really taken a beating from Brown and Karras. In the second half, Lion cornerback Dick "Night Train" Lane made a key interception, keeping the Packers from scoring. It was the Packers' only loss of the year, with a final score Green Bay 14, Detroit 26. But the Packers still became NFL champions that year.

The game was memorable for me for another reason. In the second quarter, Green Bay kicked the ball for an extra point, following a touchdown by Paul Hornung. The kick was good. The ball bounced against the facing of the second deck and came to rest on the stadium floor near my feet. I dove to the floor and hugged the ball. Several people piled on top of me. Jim Spence beat them off, pushing and pounding on them with his fists. It wasn't easy capturing the ball, but the retrieval was fast, and the struggle was definitely worthwhile.

I took pride in the football I caught that day—a great souvenir of a classic game. Years later I presented the ball to my eldest son, Bill, also a Lions fan. He secured it in a glass enclosure display case and has kept it all these years.

When It Rains, It Pours

Tilly Kaiser was a medical school graduate from Germany. She wanted further training in the United States and was accepted into a first-year residency program in internal medicine at Harper Hospital in Detroit.

Before moving to the States, Tilly wrote a letter to the hospital administrators. She had a very unusual request about her living quarters. In the letter, she stated quite simply that she did not want any room unless it had a douche. She was used to having a douche every morning, she said. She felt better if she douched. Tilly explained that she would have to turn down the residency program if her wishes were not accommodated. The matter was turned over to a high-level administrator in the hospital.

This matter soon became a gossip item among the nurses. They exclaimed, "Who does she think she is? Does she think we're going to be opening up a brothel here?" Meanwhile, the hospital administrator replied curtly to Tilly's request. He wrote, "We have plenty of female residents, Miss Kaiser. They have high standards, and they don't need a douche."

Tilly wrote back, asserting that her moral standards were just as high as anybody's and that all she wanted was a douche. This matter finally came to the attention of the chief administrator of the hospital, Dr. Aaron Tibble.

One day a lab technician, Heinrich Zoff, a former resident of Germany, approached Dr. Tibble. Zoff said, "Pardon me sir. Could I have a private word with you?" The administrator agreed. They sat down in his office. Zoff looked serious and spoke in a soft, slow voice. "In Germany we sometimes use the French word *douche* to describe a shower. It is nothing other than a bathing method, sometimes accompanied by shampoo."

The confusion was finally cleared up, to the satisfaction of both Tilly and the nurses. The matter was settled without any change in her accommodations, which already had a shower installed.

Bob and Don

D r. Bob Douglass and I met at a staff meeting at Providence Hospital and became the best of friends. We spent much time together and enjoyed each other's company. We spent many hours together, with our families, vacationing in Michigan's north country. We enjoyed teasing each other, as seen here in our correspondence concerning my promotion to chairman of the Department of OB-GYN at Providence Hospital:

January 28, 1976

Don R. Krohn, M.D.
Dept. of Obstetrics and Gynecology
Providence Hospital
16001 Nine Mile Road
Southfield, Michigan 48075

Dear Don,

As you know, I have thus far furnished you (gratuitously) a suitable theme for your position (from HMS Pinafore) since you have assumed the position as Chief. I have, of course, received scant applause and little praise for this effort.

Despite this, after a long search, I can now furnish you a suitable motto for your office. This can be framed, if necessary, and hung above your desk. It is as follows: "Many people reach the top of the tree because they lack the qualifications to detain them at the bottom."

Best regards,
Bob

February 2, 1976

Robert C. Douglass, M.D.
Internal Medicine, Endocrinology, and Philosophy
23077 Greenfield Road
Suite 250
Southfield, Michigan 48705

Dear Bob,

Your efforts to provide a suitable theme for my position have not gone unnoticed. As a matter of fact, the statement of Ustinov's that, "Many people reach the top of the tree because they lack the qualifications to detain them at the bottom," has prompted me to consider seriously, and then subsequently reject the implication that such individuals might lack the basic anchoring roots of knowledge for their position and be so full of hot air that they naturally gravitate to the top. No, again I say no. What Ustinov really implies is that those individuals with the overriding qualifications of farsightedness must necessarily find a perch from which they may utilize this talent. Thus, it is not their lack of qualifications in general but their great single virtue of striving for the overview and the recognition of this talent by their fellows who direct their progress.

If this explanation does not suffice, the remark of Dr. Johnson might well apply, "I have found you an argument, I am not obliged to find you an understanding."

Best regards,
Don R. Krohn, M.D.
Chairman, Department of Obstetrics and
Gynecology
Educational director of the Residency Program
BS, MD, FACOG, OCMC, MSMS, MSOG,
AFS, ABOG, HLCD*

*Humble Little Country Doctor

The Empress of Soul and the Arrival of Shanga Ali

One night while I was covering the obstetrical practice of an associate physician, Gene Otlewski, I was called at home by the charge nurse. She informed me that one of Otlewski's patients was in labor. I prescribed routine orders, jumped out of bed, dressed, and headed to the hospital.

When I arrived at the hospital, the atmosphere was unusual. There was much buzzing around. The nurses were talking in quiet tones and pointing to the labor room, where the patient was being initially evaluated. I asked how the patient was doing, and the nurse responded, "Well, she is doing alright, but I don't know about you. Why haven't you asked questions about the patient? After all, she's Gladys Knight!"

I said, "Who is Gladys Knight?"

She shook her head in dismay. "You haven't heard of Gladys Knight and the Pips?" she asked. "Gladys Knight is one of the most popular Motown singers. They have granted her a place of honor in every category of singing. She is a beautiful lady and has a command of music and singing that is probably unequaled. I am appalled that you don't think more of her than you apparently do!"

After being scolded by the nurse, I saw several of my patients in the hospital and acquired information from the other nurses about their favorite Gladys Knight songs, such as "Midnight Train to Georgia" and "I Heard It Through the Grapevine."

When I went in to see Gladys, she and I got along very well. She asked good questions. I soon delivered a ten-pound, twenty-three-inch baby boy. When I saw the healthy size of the baby, I said, "Gladys, it looks like you have another Pip!"

Gladys and her husband, Barry Hankerson (executive aide to then Detroit mayor Coleman Young), named the new baby Shanga Ali. I later discovered that the name means "exalted leader warrior."

Gladys and Shanga Ali did well in the hospital. Gladys was beloved by the nurses, who saw her as a very caring and mature person. The Pips visited her in the hospital. I met several of them while making patient rounds.

The evening after the birth of Shanga Ali, I sat down at the dinner table with my wife and four teenage children. I asked, "So have you kids heard of Gladys Knight?"

"Well, yeah!" they all exclaimed. "Why?"

"I delivered her baby today," I replied. As teenagers, they were stunned and very impressed by their father's brush with a celebrity. They couldn't wait to tell their friends. They also couldn't believe I hadn't previously heard of Gladys Knight. (Note, this wasn't the first time this sort of thing had happened. I hadn't recognized Marvin Gaye at first when I delivered his wife's baby.)

My youngest daughter, Kathy, asked if I could get an autograph for her.

The next day I asked Gladys for an autographed photograph. Kathy was delighted when I brought home a large postcard photo with a personal note from Gladys Knight.

Later, the OB-GYN Department received a thank-you note from Gladys about the excellent care she had received from the doctor and nurses during childbirth.

To Kathy —
As always —
Gladys Knight
& The Pips
1976

P.S. (THANK YOUR FATHER AGAIN FOR ME
FOR TAKING SUCH GOOD CARE.)

SIDNEY A. SEIDENBERG, INC. DIRECTION-MANAGEMENT 1414 AVENUE OF THE AMERICAS, NEW YORK 10019

Into Thin Air

Teamsters Union boss Jimmy Hoffa was probably feeling good about things on the drive from his home in Bloomfield Hills, Michigan, to the Machus Red Fox Restaurant, where he apparently had an appointment at 2:00 p.m. on July 30, 1975. He was to meet with two Mafia leaders, but he probably put those thoughts aside and perhaps began to reminisce about the many good times he had had at the Machus Red Fox.

Hoffa was perhaps intrigued by the red velvet tapestries, tall leather booths, and paintings that adorned the walls of the restaurant—scenes of the English hunt. In the scenes, the wily fox runs to evade the hounds. The hounds are directed in turn by a hunt master, who blows a large horn in the direction of the fox. This encourages the hounds to keep a deep scent of the fox in mind as they chase it over hill and dale. One gets the idea from observing this scene that the hounds are not as smart as the fox, especially when the fox performs a doubling-back maneuver that confuses the hounds.

Inside the Machus Red Fox, with seating for 270 guests, the booths were dimly lit. The restaurant served an imaginative surf-and-turf menu, with many seafood and red meat selections such as rack of lamb a la Leopold, veal scaloppine a la Francaise, and baked Boston scrod—all turned out by master chefs. The clientele, for the most part, were well-to-do and sophisticated. The service was excellent, and the overall atmosphere was that of a tony restaurant.

Hoffa had eaten there multiple times (his son's wedding reception was even held there) and enjoyed every meal he had had, always looking forward to the next one. However, on that day things did not work out as he had planned.

By 2:45 p.m., it was apparent to Hoffa that he had been stood up by the two Tonys—namely, Tony Giacolone (aka Tony Jack) and Tony Provenzano (aka Tony Pro). The meeting had been arranged by parties that he probably didn't know.

Hoffa became angry. He headed across the parking lot to a pay phone, apparently to prevent his conversation from being overheard. He called his wife, Josephine, and asked her if Tony Jack had phoned. When she said no, he told his wife he would be coming home around 4 p.m. to grill steaks for dinner. Josephine noted that Jimmy seemed more nervous than usual. Hoffa reportedly also called his good friend Louis Linteau, owner of an airport limousine service. In an angry tone, he told his friend that Tony Jack had stood him up.

The events to follow were recorded by witnesses on the scene. Shortly after leaving the phone booth, Hoffa got into a car and occupied the middle of the rear seat. Witnesses testified that he was not forced in any direction or into the car. He seemed to walk freely, without any evidence of fisticuffs or aggressive gestures of any kind.

On the way out of the parking lot, the driver sped away and made an illegal turn in front of a moving van, almost hitting it. The driver of the van reacted quickly and prevented an accident—although that might have saved Hoffa's life. The car drove away, and that was the last anyone ever heard from or saw Jimmy Hoffa.

While all these events were transpiring, I was inside the Machus Red Fox, meeting with three other physicians from Providence Hospital about a young surgeon we were considering appointing to the staff. The doctor, Thomas Kornmesser, the brother of my partner, had just completed a fellowship in vascular surgery, and we had an opening for a vascular surgeon at Providence.

The meeting included Dr. Jack Pfeifer, the hospital's chief of surgery, Dr. Shun Jung, education director for the surgical section, Dr. James Kornmesser (Thomas's brother), associate chairman of the OB-GYN Department, and myself, the chief of OB-GYN. We were all impressed with Thomas, who had a positive attitude about his profession. We agreed that the young man should be recommended positively to our search committee. We then left the restaurant.

Several weeks later, the FBI individually interviewed all of us. An FBI agent came to my office and asked multiple questions. "Did you see or hear Jimmy Hoffa at the restaurant?" he asked.

"No," I answered.

"Did you see or hear Jimmy Hoffa in the parking lot?"

Again my answer was no. The FBI agent told me that we had left the Machus Red Fox less than five minutes after Hoffa was seen by the group of witnesses in the parking lot.

He then asked, "Would you recognize Jimmy Hoffa if you saw him?"

"Yes," I replied. Hoffa had been a central figure in Detroit politics for years. Of course I would have recognized him. But I hadn't seen a thing. My colleagues and I all agreed that we had seen nothing unusual occur at the Red Fox that day.

I later read that the day after Hoffa's disappearance, the police from Bloomfield Township had come to the restaurant to investigate. They had found Hoffa's car, a "massively large" green Pontiac convertible. The car was unlocked. There was no extensive search of the car at that time.

The FBI became involved in the case two or three days later and spent the next ten years actively investigating Hoffa's disappearance. He was declared legally dead in 1982, seven years after his disappearance.

Jimmy Hoffa's troubles began in 1964, when he was convicted by a federal court in Chattanooga, Tennessee. He was sentenced to a fifteen-year prison term for jury tampering and for misusing union pension funds. Hoffa appealed the ruling for three years but finally began serving his jail term. After serving approximately four years, he was pardoned by President Richard Nixon, who stipulated that Hoffa refrain from any active participation in or leadership of the Teamsters Union.

Hoffa had hand-picked his successor, Frank Fitzsimons, who by all accounts was acceptable to both Nixon and the Mafia. They all got along well, which hadn't been the case with Hoffa. Many people objected to Hoffa's pardon, and it's no wonder that many parties were upset when Hoffa tried again to run for Teamsters president. However, the Teamsters remained quite loyal to Hoffa.

Looking back on these events, many questions remain. One of the most intriguing is: What happened to Hoffa's body? Authorities have made several attempts to find the body and have investigated various sites. According to one allegation, Hoffa's body was buried in a barn with a dirt floor. Investigators brought a front-end loader into the barn and dug up the floor. But no trace of human remains was found. Another story says that Hoffa's body was placed in a steel drum and frozen. Yet another says the body was encased in concrete and dropped in one of the Great Lakes. Cremation was another theory. Probably the most bizarre theory was that the body was ground up and added to various meat products, such as hamburgers, hotdogs, and salami. All in all, there has been a lot of conflicting testimony and several confessions, but to this day no one knows what happened to his body. Whether Hoffa was indeed murdered, and if so how, remains a mystery.

Perhaps it is time, even at this late date, to conduct this investigation with a special prosecutor. In the 1960s, Bobby Kennedy and Jimmy Hoffa were bitter enemies, and perhaps there was a political overtone to the whole issue. It seems strange to me that the FBI, which was called in early in the case, was not more successful in obtaining indictment material. The fact is that the FBI was outsmarted by the Mafia.

It seems strange to me that a man so rich, powerful, and well known could vanish into thin air. Yet this is apparently what happened.

James Riddle Hoffa with his son James Phillip Hoffa at a testimonial dinner in 1965

Ten Years on a Farm

I have been influenced by *Mother Earth News* and other publications concerning environmental threats. These threats include air pollution and contamination of streams, rivers, groundwater, and other drinking water. Farmers use biologically active medications such as steroids and antibiotics to promote rapid weight gain and tissue growth in animals. Construction materials such as lead and asbestos have proven to be deadly. Offshore oil drilling dominates the news of the day and appears to be a significant threat. Carcinogens, disposal of nuclear materials, plain garbage, and gases and compounds that evolve in dumps are other environmental problems. Even space is becoming more and more treacherous as people launch more satellites, which occasionally strike each other. Research shows that a huge satellite might even crash into a major city.

The environmental threats we face on a worldwide basis are nearly overwhelming. Yet they are so common that we often fail to pay attention to them. Health problems caused by exposure to pollutants are preventable. I believe we should pay more attention to our basic health needs and invest more in scientific research that seeks to better identify the threats.

How do we fight environmental threats and protect our health? For an individual, self-sufficiency is one approach. For society as a group, one approach is to make laws that discourage behavior and practices that threaten the environment. Here is a comparison of the two approaches:

Don R. Krohn, M.D.

INDIVIDUAL EFFORT	GROUP EFFORT
Independent	Societal
Personal	Impersonal
Change is easier	Change is more difficult
Ego	Id
Degrees of change	No degrees of change
Review of results is clear	Review of results is biased and unclear
Personal challenge	Political challenge

Political unrest and nuclear terrorism are important considerations in this regard. In regard to self-sufficiency, I think it can be adequately stated that it is impossible to be completely self-sufficient in today's world. I submit that it would be better to think in degrees of self-sufficiency, especially in those ways that would lead to more continual improvement.

***

In the 1970s, Betty and I became interested in the self-sufficient lifestyle. In discussing what we thought we might do, we developed a preliminary plan. This plan might be helpful to anybody interested in the self-sufficient lifestyle or the activity of the small farmer:

1. Continually increase knowledge base. This is probably the most important prerequisite because it covers so much of the problem in an ongoing manner.

2. Obtain aerial photographic surveys of properties you are considering buying to evaluate the suitability for the desired farming operations. These surveys show property boundaries and water runoff from surrounding properties.

3. Provide a water collection and irrigation system.

4. Develop a garden with southern exposure and protection from wind. Plan on spending time on continued ridding of weeds from the garden area.

5. Take soil samples. To grow crops, you must be aware of the balance of nutrients in the soil, as you may have to supplement the nutrients.

6. Find a local veterinary service that specializes in large animals to ensure the health of animals under your care. Investigate local health problems of farm animals to prevent problems with your animals.

7. Take a Master Gardener's course to get up-to-date information on the local climate and soil.

8. Maintain continued contact with agricultural officials on local, state, and national levels.

9. Construct a fish pond for food and for recreation. Consult state Department of Natural Resources officials and read DNR instructions and regulations concerning appropriate placement.

10. Own and breed beef cattle. This will require fencing.

11. Secure facilities, such as a barn and shed for tools and a tractor.

12. Annually review the successes and failures of the operation.

One of the most urgent requisites is that the plan be implemented.

We looked at real estate listings and picked a twenty-acre parcel with a three-bedroom house and a barn for hay storage. The house had a see-through fireplace that heated two rooms, making wood heat a practical application. The property had a spring-fed stock pond, adequate pasture and garden space, and beautiful walnut trees at the back. The irrigation system left much to be desired, but we decided it was repairable. The thirty-five-minute commute to my OB-GYN office was a problem, but my business partners made concessions on coverage of patient care after business hours (a frequent occurrence in our specialty). Our neighbors were also very friendly and helpful.

The next step was to create an implementation plan suitable to the goals of the particular farming operation selected. The plan must be flexible, as compromise might be needed. For example, equipment may need to be rented instead of purchased. As part of our implementation plan, Betty earned a Master Gardner's certificate at Michigan State University. We also acquired the following at local auctions:

> Serviceable 35-horsepower tractor with a three-point
>   hitch and live power
> Mower-crimper
> Plow
> Cultivator
> Baler
> Hay wagon
> Rake
> Fencing and supplies with controller
> Hand tools
> Garden supplies

Freezer
Eight beef cattle (plan ahead for bull services and for
   calving 280 days later)

We found a neighbor knowledgeable about farm equipment. He helped me determine the value and serviceability of the
items being auctioned.

Implementation also involved getting the irrigation system
working. Our system had a line that went from the spring-fed
pond to a pump to a line under the barn to the four or five sprin-
kler heads that watered the garden. The garden was about ten
feet above the level of the spring pond.

We also had to construct the fish pond. We hired a local
contractor, who dug our pond per state DNR instructions and
regulations. The state provided fish, including bluegills, channel
catfish, and bass, for a nominal fee. These fish were compatible
for the most part, as they did not eat each other.

***

The results of our farming experience were mostly positive.
The fish in our pond showed excellent growth, with the average
length of catfish at twenty-two inches. The bass and bluegills
prospered as well. The fish gave us the satisfying recreational activity of catching and releasing them. We used worms and barb-
less hooks. I had wanted to raise chickens, but Betty preferred
to devote her time to gardening and other domestic responsibili-
ties. We decided to raise geese, which worked out well except
that after three years, we had thirty geese. (We had planned to
only have five or six.) The geese turned out to be an unsuccess-
ful poultry-raising attempt. We also enjoyed the sandhill cranes
that lived on our property. In a sense, they provided an aesthetic

approximation of poultry on the farm. We had a bumper crop of garden vegetables, including beans, lettuce, strawberries, asparagus, and sweet corn. We felt profound satisfaction from our successes in vegetable, beef, and hay production.

Our youngest daughter, Kathy, was about to start her senior year of high school when we moved to the farm. We expected the move to be hard for her, but soon after changing schools, she made a lot of friends and took up an interest in journalism. This interest led her to the University of Michigan, where she majored in communications.

There are things I would have done differently. I would produce maple syrup as a matter of self-sufficiency rather than as a hobby. I would also grow fruit trees. I would continue with wood heat but would get an efficient woodstove or fireplace insert.

I advise that the chimney be cleaned a minimum of once a year, at the beginning of the heating season. One fall day, while I was at work, our neighbor called and asked Betty, "Do you know there is a ten-foot flame shooting from the top of your chimney?" We were very grateful to the volunteer fire department, which came quickly and saved our house.

Betty, our son David, and I harvest hay for winter storage.
The farm family gets a real understanding of the meaning of
pride.

Don R. Krohn, M.D.

The fish pond under construction, with my daughter-in-law
Cynthia, wife Betty, daughter Kathy, and our dog Cindy

A mother cow and calf enjoy life on the farm.

Vignette: The Pond

It had been two weeks since it had rained. The filter at the inlet of the irrigation pipe to the pasture was clogged up, threatening the garden crops and animals. I needed to unclog the filter at once.

The day was hot and humid. I knew there would be a problem with the thousands of mosquitoes that swarmed around the pond and made whining, angry, high-pitched sounds as they circled about. The noise they made was a constant reminder of their ability to bite and cause mischief.

Betty and my daughter-in-law Patty helped me dress as carefully as possible. Pant cuffs filled the upper part of my boots. A long-sleeved heavy shirt, gloves, a hat, and a tight collar around my neck seemed to do the trick. Betty and Patty double-wrapped me in mosquito netting and tied it in a knot behind my back.

I went to the barn and hauled out a flat-bottomed rowboat, which was quite ancient and had been left there by a previous owner. Under the boat, I found a half-rotten oar, which I used to steer. After getting to the center of the pond, where the inlet valve was located, I leaned over and successfully unclogged the filter. I relaxed, apparently slumped, and went right overboard as the flat-bottomed rowboat capsized. I somehow wound up with the boat over me. My head was in an air pocket, and I took a deep breath.

As it turned out, the water was only about five feet deep. I was able to walk to shore. I emerged from the pond covered with slime and decaying malodorous matter.

I headed to the house. Betty and Patty, seeing my predicament, came out to help. They looked shocked at first but relaxed when they found out I was okay. I became quite angry with the knot holding my outfit together. It was behind me, giving me no way to reach back and untie it. Patty and Betty helped with this, and I got out of my slimy getup—after which we all had a good laugh.

Later, Patty fashioned a toy bear and dressed it to resemble the way I looked on the day I fell into the pond. It has been sitting in our house on display ever since, and I take this opportunity to give Patty credit for making this little fashion plate.

The filter never clogged again. Apparently this was a one-time phenomenon that occurred when vegetation had grown excessively in the spring.

This dapper little man sets the standard for pond-side attire in the war against mosquitoes.

Vignette: Poultry

We had Black Angus cattle, a fishpond, a donkey, a dog, and cats. Now I thought we needed poultry. My friend Larry Gilson and I drew up the plans and started digging the foundation for a chicken house. I was well into the project when Betty came running from the garden. She quickly told us that she was not going to take care of chickens then or ever. She had already done that when she was young. I liked the idea and the planning but did not recognize the time required for feeding, watering, collecting eggs, and cleaning out manure.

Instead we decided to get a pair of nice white geese. In about three years, they had multiplied to thirty nice white geese. They were fine as long as they were fenced. To keep them fenced, we needed to trim their wings annually, which was a two-person task. I worked long hours forty miles from home and had no time for wing trimming. The wings grew; the geese flew. Over the fence they went, to mess on the driveway, sidewalk, porches, and anywhere else they chose to go.

When it was time for the geese to go to market, I took them in my pickup truck, which had a canopy over the bed. There was enough room for twelve geese. I knew they would fight, so I tied each goose's feet together to prevent chaos in the back of my truck. I drove twenty-five miles or so to the goose auction.

A young boy met me at the gate and asked for money to help me unload my geese. I opened the back of the truck to see a mess. They had all become untied. I was glad to have the boy's help and a water hose nearby. The geese sold for just enough to pay for my gas for the trip and the boy's help.

By the time I got home and showered, I was tired and sick from the mess. Betty said we would clean up the truck when I felt better. I went to sleep. While I was napping, Betty's mother, Lydia, came by. She looked at the open truck and said, "Honey, we had better clean up this mess. Don is sick." I had a great mother-in-law! That was the end of my poultry endeavor.

Laying the foundation for the chicken coop, moments before
Betty intercepted me

Vignette: Sandhill Cranes

One of the first springs on the farm, Betty and I were sitting on the porch, watching our cows and newborn calves grazing in the back pasture. Suddenly, two giant birds—four and a half to five feet tall, with six- to seven-foot wingspans—flew in and landed in our pasture. We identified them as sandhill cranes. They had a stately upright stance, with long necks, heavy straight bills, long legs, and "bustles" of tertial feathers drooping over their tails. Their plumage was gray, but it appeared rusty because of iron stains from the water in tundra ponds.

The two cranes performed a nuptial dance soon after their arrival: they circled each other around and around, jumping up in the air in a kind of bouncing display. As they circled, their long necks intertwined. Then they bowed to each other and repeated the performance, uttering raucous croaking calls. They then walked into the cornfield and marsh. We saw them again in about six weeks, when they brought their two chicks into the pasture.

Female sandhill cranes lay one to two eggs in large mounds of grass and uprooted plants in undisturbed marshes. Both males and the females tend to the nests and feed their young. Prehistoric birds, sandhill cranes are monogamous and are said to mate for life. They migrate in flocks. They will return each year to a particular area, which in our case was a swamp located at the posterior edge of our property. I think possibly we were seeing the same pair each year.

The sandhill crane, a magnificent prehistoric bird

Plaqueless

A l Gore was elected vice president of the United States in 1992, on the ticket with Bill Clinton. Early in Clinton's presidency, Al and his wife, Tipper, decided to take a two-week vacation. They planned to stay in a large, two-story, eight-room log cabin that overlooked beautiful Center Hill Lake in Smithville, Tennessee, near Al's hometown of Carthage. (Al and his father, who had served as both a congressional representative and a senator from Tennessee, also had extensive land holdings near Carthage.) The log cabin was located at the end of the road that Betty and I then lived on.

A group of about twenty Secret Service agents was assigned to protect the vice president. These individuals were to stay with him day and night while they maintained surveillance of cars in our small subdivision.

The Secret Service did much preliminary work before Al's arrival. For example, they needed a place for the aboveground septic tank of a Winnebago, which was to house some of the agents for two weeks. They chose a spot on the corner of our neighbor Joe's property, about a quarter mile from Gore's rental house. Joe was upset that they would put a tank so close to his house; there were a lot of other places they could have chosen. Joe raised hell about it and wouldn't let them park their trailer and equipment on his property.

I was mowing the grass one day when a Secret Service agent approached me. Explaining his problem, he asked, "Would you allow us to park on your property and put the hot phone, the red phone that connects to the White House, and all its equipment in your basement?"

I responded, "Well, I didn't vote for the man, but I respect the office of the vice president, and I think he is entitled to protection. So I will say yes; you can use my home." They were my friends from the minute I said that until the minute they left.

Stationed in our basement for two weeks, they talked with me on several occasions. They all spoke poorly of Al Gore. They didn't like his "highfalutin" ways, and they thought he was a fake. I had dinner with one of the agents in Nashville. He told me all kinds of things that had happened while he worked for Al Gore. He remarked that Al was nasty to the Secret Service on several occasions.

For exercise, Al jogged out to the main road and back, about a mile round-trip, virtually every day. When Betty and I were sitting on our porch, we would see him go by, sometimes with Tipper and one of their daughters. On most occasions, he was dressed very casually and appeared to be enjoying himself.

Because he appreciated our "service to the country," our housing the Secret Service and all, the head agent said he was going to call Donna Brazile, Al's campaign manager and confidant. He would have Donna contact me, he said, and I would receive a plaque commemorating the fact that I had housed the Secret Service, had been hospitable, and had gone out of my way to help them protect the vice president.

Well, they never sent the damned thing. Before they left, they did give me a pen with Gore's name on it, and they gave Betty a garden hoe that they had used to kill rattlesnakes in the dense foliage on the bluff.

***

I have another story concerning Al Gore. Betty and I went in to buy a recliner at D. T. McCall & Sons, a well-known furniture and appliance store in Carthage. Two Danish reporters were in the aisle next to us. The owner, McCall himself, was talking with them. At the time, McCall owned a truck that advertised bad news about Al Gore. McCall told the reporters that Al Gore had buried environmental pollutants on his farm.

McCall said, "He would tell everybody else about global warming and environmental problems, and he's going to go ahead and contaminate his own damn farm."

The reporter looked shocked. "You mean to tell me that here in the hometown of Al Gore, people don't like him?" he asked. "I thought he was one of your favorite politicians!"

McCall responded, "I wouldn't vote for that son of a [bleep] if he ran for dog catcher."

Al Gore and family stroll past our Tennessee home in 1993.

About the Author

Don R. Krohn, M.D., was born in Bloomfield, Nebraska, in 1929. His family moved to Detroit in the early 1940s. Krohn later left home to attend boarding school in Indiana. After graduation, he enrolled at Wayne State University in Detroit, where he met his future wife, Betty Jo, in 1949.

Krohn attended medical school at the University of Michigan in Ann Arbor, interned at Bronson Methodist Hospital in Kalamazoo, and served his residency at Harper Hospital in Detroit. In 1959 he was called to service in the U.S. Air Force. He and his family moved to Bitburg, Germany. A captain, Krohn worked for two years as an obstetrician and gynecologist at Bitburg Air Force Base Hospital.

While he and Betty raised four children, Krohn worked as an OB-GYN in the suburban Detroit area. For fourteen years, he served as a director of the Residency Training Program and chairman of the Obstetrics and Gynecology Department at Providence Hospital in Southfield, Michigan.

In 1988 Dr. Krohn and Betty relocated to her hometown of Smithville, Tennessee. Over the next eight years, Krohn served on the faculty of the Vanderbilt University Medical Center and the University of Tennessee in Chattanooga.

Dr. Krohn released his first book of humorous, real-life stories, *Tap Dancing, Babies, and Cadavers: Humor and Pathos in the Life of a 20th-Century Doctor*, in 2009. He has been profiled in the *Eugene Register-Guard* and by the University of Oregon.

Don R. Krohn, M.D.

Tap Dancing, Babies, and Cadavers is included in the historical collections of the Detroit Public Library, Wayne State University, the Bloomfield (Nebraska) Historical Society, and the Nebraska State Historical Society. The book is also in the history library and archives of the American College of Obstetricians and Gynecologists in Washington, D.C.

Dr. Krohn and his family now live in Eugene, Oregon. He can be contacted at donkrohn@gmail.com.

Photo Credits

Made in the USA
San Bernardino, CA
15 June 2018